First publ

b

GW01406733

The Kiddywin]
180 Gla:
G81 ₁QQ
Scotland

ISBN   0 9519836 0 1

Printed by John McCormick & Co Ltd
74 Buchanan Street
Glasgow G1 3HE

" *There comes a moment*

when you realise progress

and new technology is

entering your daily life

like an express train . .

and you've not even

purchased a ticket "

The Authors Thoughts . . .

Many articles and publications have been presented to the
general public in recent years, explaining how to use the
modern Personal Computer, how it works, and describing
its system of operation. All have, in my experience,
made the classic mistake of giving the reader " TOO MUCH,
TOO SOON ". . . . . Many authors have also fallen down
the " Literary Hole " by showing off their in-depth
knowledge and expertise of the subject matter, which only
gives the average *soon to be user*, a blinding headache, a
twitching sensation in his or her central nervous system
and sweaty palms. . when in all reality . . .

ALL THEY WANT TO DO IS SIT DOWN IN

FRONT OF THE BLASTED THING WITH A

MODICUM OF CONFIDENCE AND A MINIMUM

OF TECHNICAL KNOWLEDGE .

THE MORE MINIMUM THE BETTER !

Without insulting anyones intelligence and denied the
benefit of a one to one teaching situation and
assessment, the entry level of teaching the subject has
to be (as our American cousins would say) *right on the
bottom line.* Comparators will have to be used, analogies
presented, and everyday interpretations used as much as
possible and more to the point, good old fashioned plain
language used. When some technical knowledge is given,
this will be as simple and as concise as possible, you
have my word on that !

There are many college courses, evening classes, magazine
articles, and publications dedicated to the Personal
Computer and its use, so if you desire to improve your
knowledge there is no excuse, but at least after drinking
from this little font of instruction, you'll have a
fighting chance of understanding them without blowing
your brains, nerves, and confidence to shreds !

A nice side effect is also understanding a little of what
the *office genius* is prattling on about as he or she
preens their feathers of knowledge.

" *Now enter the 1990's with a*
gentle push and the train ticket
firmly clasped in your hand "

BEFORE WE BEGIN . . . . . . .A LITTLE STORY !

(for those of you who like little stories)

WE'VE PASSED THIS WAY BEFORE

In the 1930's 40's and 50's those of us earning our daily
crust in an office or suchlike departments which dealt
with the all important administration of a business,
would recognise Florence. She was the number one person
o.k. had her own desk, usually up front where everyone
could see her (something about corporate image the boss
said). Not for her the filing cabinets or any menial
tasks, oh no, she had this " latest model " typewriter on
her desk. The boss always remarked that with his new
design of stationary and a well typed letter the firms
image was " up there ", whatever that meant. We used to
watch Florence show off her skills on that machine every
day, " 100 words a minute ", " First in her college
exam ", we heard it till our ears fell off !

" Save valuable time and money ", " An efficient typist
can reduce your office overheads ", screamed the adverts
for these things. Rather ominous thought I.

Strange looking machines they were too, mostly black with
chrome bits on, a lot of strange bits and bobs on them
too, such as a Tabulator Key ; a Platen ; a Carriage
Return Lever ; a Space Bar, some even had a little bell !
I was really shook up when I visited other businesses in
our little town whilst delivering some of our office
mail, these things were breeding, one and two were
appearing in places where previously there had been none
They weren't all identical mind you, and they had names
like Adler ; Olivetti ; Underwood ; Royal ; Olympia and
Imperial. We even heard that an electric one was on the
way !

The peculiar thing I did notice though was the keyboards,
they all looked similar, QWERTY or something. I sat
down in front of Florence's one day when she was off and
had a bash at it, made a right mess of using it I did.
Do you know she told me next day that someone had been
touching it ? As if I would, said I !

I realised that if I wanted to get better paid, like
Florence, I would have to learn to operate one of those
things, if you can't beat them, join them. After two
years at night classes in our local school I passed my
exams and now have a well paid job like Florence.

Florence's actually.

SOME ? YEARS LATER . . . .

Who said retirement ?

I'm working part time for a local builders merchant, a
friend of my husbands, it's only for three days a week
and it's going to help with the finance for a holiday
visit to my eldest son in Canada next year. This man has
just bought one of these Personal Computer things, P.C.
he calls it, says it will save him hours of work in
ordering and stocktaking with this special database
program in it. Its also got a word processing program in
it as well, which makes this P.C. do everything a
typewriter can do and more, so he's given me his old
typewriter for the neighbours children to play with.
These P.C.'s are getting very popular I'm thinking, even
the local chemist has got one ! They all look much the
same as well but the names are different Olivetti ;
Packard Bell ; IBM ; Tika ; Apricot ; Reeves ; Goldstar ;
Dell ; Austin,   amongst others.

They all have little T.V. screens, mostly in colour, on
top of their box, the keyboards are separate though,
which is a useful idea. The one thing that amused me
though was that the old faithful QWERTY keyboard is still
being used, although it appears to have a lot of special
keys on it as well, and I noticed a Numeric Keypad for
figure only entries, very handy that I would imagine.
Oh dear, Cursor keys ; CTRL keys ; Function keys ;
delete ; end ; page up ; page down ; an Alt key ? There
are some strange ones here ! Well, here we go again says
I, only this time I've got this little book to save my
blushes as I learn. . . . . .

They tell me some makes can do more tricks than others
but they cost more ! Reminds me of a typewriter salesman
I met once . . . .

v

PART 1

enough information for you
to break the door down !

THE   HARDWARE

is

the **Jargon** for all the units and extras that
make up the complete personal computer system.

n.b.   **JARGON**   a noun,   used to describe words
or expressions developed for use within a particular
group, hard for outsiders to understand.

There are examples of Jargon throughout this book to
make you sound as good as the " guys and gals " around
you !

P.C. ?

it's   the " **jargon** "   for

a   Personal   Computer.

That's All

V.D.U ?

(video display unit)

The T.V. like object on the top of your P.C.
which most people call a **Monitor.**

In recent years colour has become the " norm " and the
quality is getting exceptional, this really shows through
in the graphic displays of some programs, A *high
resolution display* is what the *office genius* prattles on
about, this simply means . . . . **your monitor picture**
is **much sharper, and the colours more vibrant.**

It's a case of, the " higher the resolution ",
the higher the capital expenditure !

Portable personal computers use a special L C D (Liquid
Crystal Display) monitor screen to let you see what's
happening, these screen displays have excellent
resolution and contrast.

Portable personal computers are called " LAPTOPS "

The Hardware

Desk Model Personal Computer

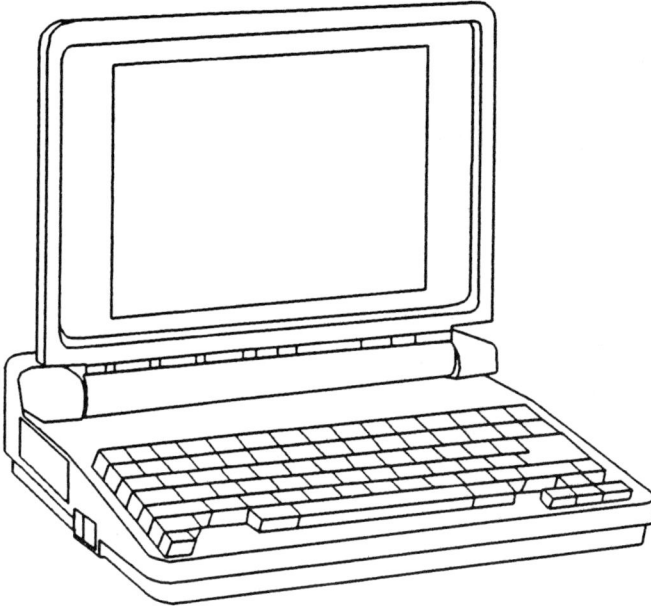

A " Laptop "   Personal Computer

On the train . . .   or on the 'plane, this is the P.C.
model for the " upwardly mobile ", these portables will
run from a mains supply socket or their own internal re-
chargeable battery pack. On average the modern laptops
will, with " power management circuits ", run for 3 to
4 hrs on one charge.

There are now portable printers being marketed to
complement the laptop P.C.'s.

Have office . . . will travel !

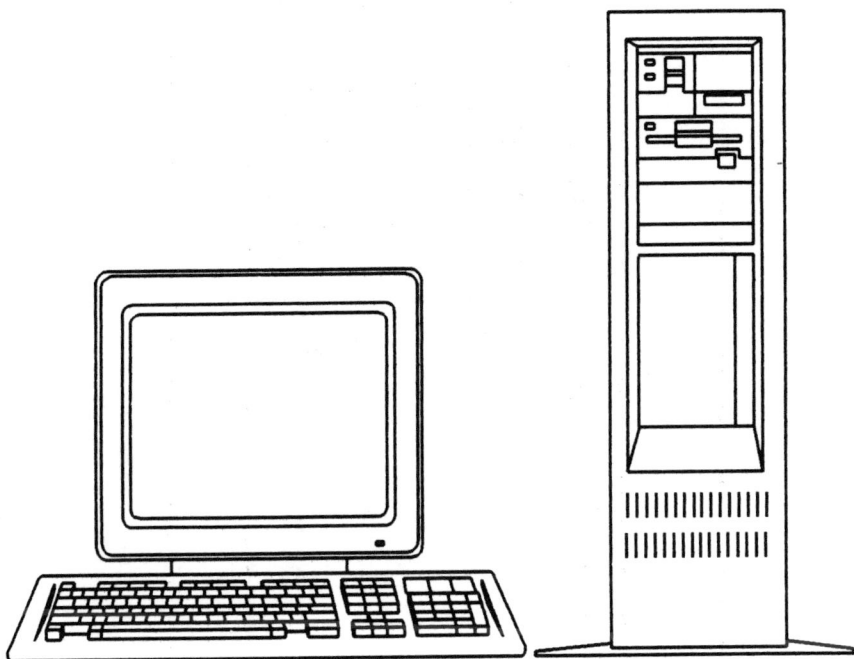

The " Tower " Model Personal Computer

In the 1940's and early 50's car radio's were bulky in
size due to the fact that they used valves instead of
transistors, so some manufacturers made the radio unit to
fit under the bonnet and only a small control panel was
fitted in the cab ! Here we have a similar idea . . . .
Only the P.C. monitor sits on your desk, the " tower "
can be sited anywhere it will be unobtrusive.

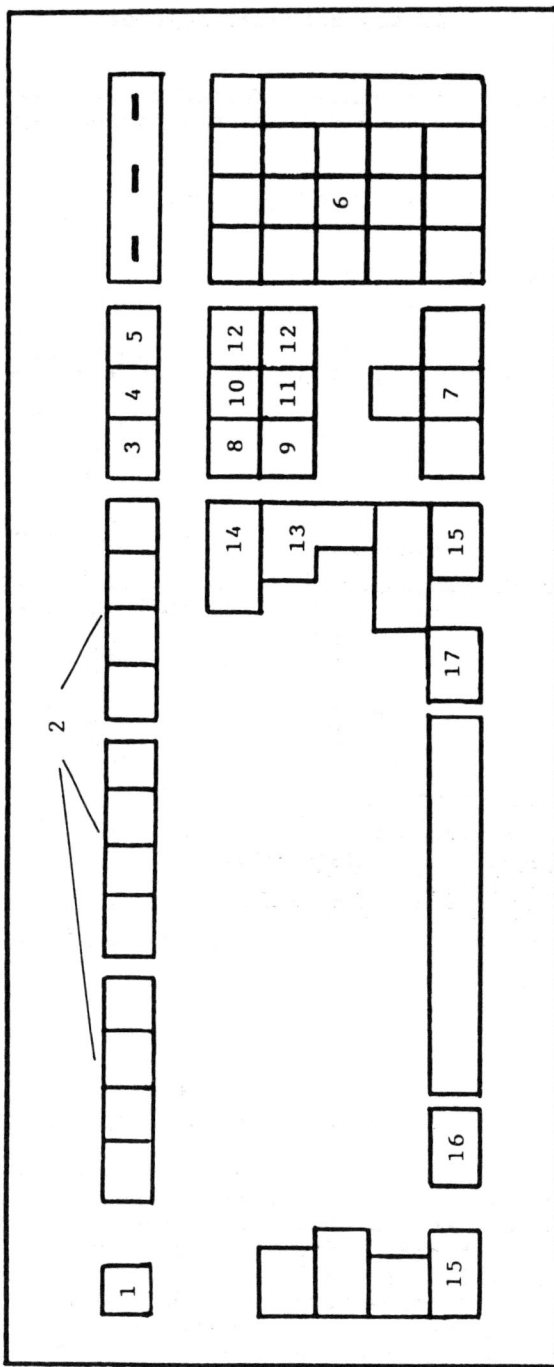

102 key Enhanced Keyboard

Keyboards with a Numeric Keypad on them are called enhanced. Modern P.C.'s have enhanced keyboards.

1   **ESCAPE KEY** If the whole program grinds to a halt, this is worth trying. **CTRL** and **BREAK** do the same.

2   **FUNCTION KEYS**   programmers use these for you to give and receive instructions in a program.

3   **PRINT SCREEN** If you see it on your monitor screen, hitting this one will print it out for you. **TEXT ONLY**

4   **SCROLL LOCK**   Stops the display moving as you scroll.

5   **PAUSE**   Time for a tea break !

6   **NUMERIC KEYPAD**   (* is MULTIPLY   / is DIVIDE)

7   **CURSOR CONTROL GROUP**   Moves the little white marker to where you want to type the **NEXT** character.

8   **INSERT**   For inserting characters into TEXT.

9   **DELETE**   An electronic rubber !

10 **HOME** Hold down CTRL and hit HOME and the cursor moves back to the start of the page.

11 **END**   Hold down CTRL and hit END and the cursor moves to the end of the page.

12 **PAGE UP** and **PAGE DOWN** Allows you to view different pages of your documentation on the monitor screen.

13 **THE ENTER KEY**

14 **BACKSPACE KEY**

15 **CTRL**   This key, used in association with others will carry out functions in a program.

16 **ALT**   This key is used to access about 120 ASCII CODE characters, refer to your P.C. manual for details about using them . . . . .
FOR EXAMPLE, **Press and hold ALT** and then hit **171** on the Numeric Key Pad, **release ALT** and you have ½   172 gives you ¼

17 **ALT.GR**   Once again a special access key for codes but can't see you ever using it.

The   Mouse

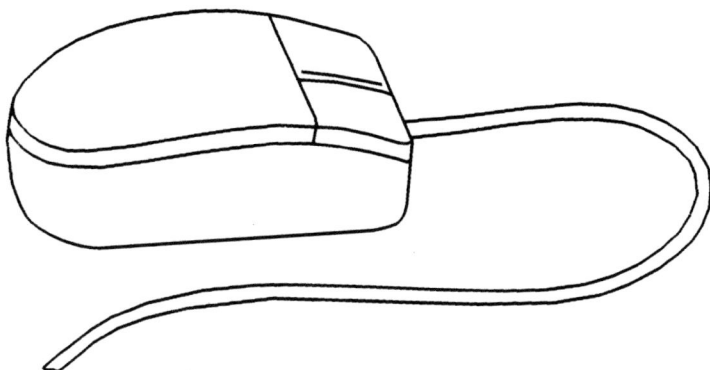

The mouse is connected to the P.C. via a special plug and
socket, (there are now infra red cordless versions on
the market !) its purpose is to allow you to move a
small white arrow around the monitor screen, point it to
words or icons on the program display, and by pressing
one or other of the two buttons, carry out that command
or function.

A LOT BETTER THAN TYPING IT OUT, EH ?

ICONS are small graphic bit pictures, describing commands
or program functions.

also . . . *Mouse mats are available from most dealers
and provide the mouse with the right sliding surface.*

Floppy Disk

The Diskette to give it its proper name, is used by the Personal Computer to record and play back **DATA**.

DATA just simply means information the P.C. understands.

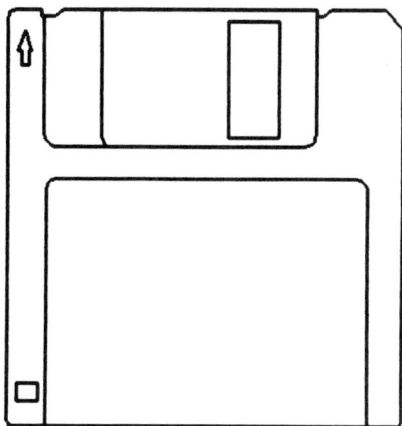

The   3½ inch   " Floppy Disk "

Not so " Floppy " now as they are inside a nice
dustproof, fingerprint proof plastic sleeve supposedly
designed to fit inside a shirt pocket. So they say !

Remember the break off tabs on the side of an audio
cassette ? They saved you recording over your favourite
music etc by mistake, didn't they ? Well the diskette,
to give it its proper name, has a similar facility, it's
called a write / protect slider and is at one corner of
the plastic sleeve. You simply select by sliding it **UP** or
DOWN.

A good way to remember this is to say **WRITE - UP** !
which allows you to put new information / data on the
disk, whilst automatically erasing the old.

The Diskettes or " Floppy Disks "

The 3½ inch comes in two capacities . . . .

first of all they have a special magnetic coating on
both sides . . .thats why the're called **Double Sided** !

The **Double Density** versions can record 720 kilobytes of
information.

The **High Density** versions can record 1.44 megabytes of
information.

The 5¼ inch also comes in two capacities . . . .

Like the 3½ inch they are **Double sided.**

The **Double Density** versions can record 360 kilobytes of
information.

The **High Density** version can record 1.2 megabytes of
information.

At this point let me explain what a **BYTE** is. A **BYTE** is
the smallest unit of data that a computer uses, it is
equivalent to you typing **2 characters on your keyboard,
also** in the P.C. world a **KILO is = to 1024 bytes** and a
MEGA is = to 1,048,576 bytes, so you can now work out the
amount of characters these disks can hold.

Another name for information is   **DATA**

There's no need to go into the technical difference of
Double or High Density, suffice to say that High Density
disks carry a lot more information and could be cheaper
to use in the long run, it really depends on what your
doing. They cost more as well, surprise surprise !

One serious point. Make sure the drive mechanism on your
P.C., (3½ inch or 5¼ inch), can take the higher
capacity disks, most machines have high capacity drive
units fitted, but its worth while checking out.

GOLDEN RULE. The disk capacity must never exceed the
drive capacity. In other words make sure your P.C. can
play **High Density** Disks before you buy them !

THE DISKS AND THEIR DRIVES

1. The Diskette and its Drive.

You should know what a " floppy disk " is by now, to use
the jargon, so no more about that ! The disk slides into
a special drive unit (3½ or 5¼) in the front of your
P.C. This drive carries out a similar task to the audio
cassette drive in your music centre or radio/cassette
recorder. Likewise, it also has *special heads* inside it,
not for record/playback and erase, but tiny *read/write*
heads, one for each side of the disk, (*remember, the
disks are double sided*). When you write, you will
automatically erase over existing data, provided the
little slider on the disk cover is in the WRITE position.

THIS DRIVE IS ALWAYS CALLED THE " A " DRIVE
no matter what make your P.C. is.

If you have an extra drive fitted, or alongside as extra
hardware, it is always known as the " B " DRIVE

1.1   The Hard Disk.

This drive unit is fitted internally into most P.C.'s,
although some manufacturers make it removable for your
security purposes, (if you have the money you can get
anything !). It's a complex electro - mechanical unit
with special rotating disk platters inside it, and yes,
it has special heads as well, for reading and for writing
data. **BUT,** its capacity for storing data is way above
that of a " floppy ", in fact it can be equivalent to
20, 30, 40, 60, 85, 110, or 240 " floppy disks " ! If
you have the money and of course the need, you can have a
biggy, it all depends on what your requirements are,
certainly some of the new programs are using a lot of
data in their make up, more than anyone would have
dreamed of 3 or 4 years ago.

Remember the old record players of the 50's and 60's ?
you could select 10 of your favourite records and stack
them on the record changer and it would play them one
after the other automatically, a lot better than playing
one at a time. Well, a Hard Disk offers you a similar
facility to keep your most used programs on, **only, you
can select which one to play** *and* **when.**

ONE ALMIGHTY FILING CABINET FOR YOUR PROGRAMS and FILES

THE HARD DISK IS CALLED THE " C " DRIVE
no matter what make of P.C. you have.

All of this saves you time and effort in throwing your most used programs in and out 5, 6 or whatever times a day.   But the facility for reading a disk without installing it on your hard drive is still there, isn't it ? **The " A " Drive** !

For example . . .   The company salesman types you a list of his calls and appointments for the month ahead on his Laptop P.C., copies it onto a disk, labels it, leaves it on your desk, and then he's off on a grand tour of Europe, (lucky guy !)

Any time you wish you can insert *his* disk in **The " A " Drive**, play it, and remind yourself of where you can leave a message for him to contact the office. (unlucky guy !).

Finally. . . . When you initially load a program into the computer you have a choice, either to always run it and close it from the " A " drive **or** install it on the Hard Disk and keep the program disk as a back-up. The choice is yours.

A LITTLE SNIPPET

Both the **" A Drive "** and the **" C Drive "** on the computer have indicator lights beside them, these are called **LEDS,** (light emitting diodes). It is normal for them to flash on and off intermittantly when you are using the drives.

ANOTHER   LITTLE   SNIPPET

When you purchase a blank audio cassette for your radio cassette or music centre, you fit it into the drive on your machine and you can make recordings on it, SIMPLE !

But when you purchase Brand New "floppy" disks for your P.C. you must *FORMAT* them before copying information on to them.

What the computer does is electronically divide the disk recording surface into sectors instead of the usual one long recording track.

This allows the P.C. to search the disk even faster for the information you are searching for.

YOU *FORMAT* A DISK ONLY ONCE, WHEN ITS NEW. Even after erasing files of information **or** copying new information on to it . . . . There's no need to *format* it again.

THERE IS A *FORMAT* COMMAND ON YOUR   DISK OPERATING SYSTEM PROGRAM, (more about that subject in   PART II)

more Jargon.

Software

The name given to programs which will run on your P.C.

A Word on Programs

Programmers or software designers write programs for your P.C. in a special language which only the electronic innards of your computer can understand. Unless you want to get " into " programming you don't want to know about it, believe me. Just like anything else in this world, you will get good and bad, some programs are easy to use and some will make you visit the old aunt you haven't seen in years ! Ask around, its the good ones that sell the best.

Just like a pre-recorded audio cassette of your favourite music or singer, you can buy programs in the disk size of your choice all ready for you to run in your P.C. It can be an **accountancy program** ; a **game** ; a **household accounts** package ; a **word processing program** (allows you to use the P.C. like a typewriter, and more), a **database**, (a program that allows you to enter information and arrange it any way you choose, for example, names and addresses ; colours styles and sizes of shoes in your stockroom) or a **spreadsheet**, which allows you to show your figures and information in columns and rows in an easy read format. You name it and in all possibility a program has been written for it !

Large corporate companies sometimes have software written and designed to suit their particular kind of work, but most buy off the shelf, especially word processing programs.

When you purchase a Personal Computer program you will usually end up with 1, 2, or more disks (depends on the size of the program) and a complex manual that also tells you how to install it in your P.C.
The technical authorship and layouts in some of these books can make you a "gibbering wreck " very quickly, so it's nice to know that programmers and software designers are providing **QUICKSTART** instructions as well as the main program manual. If you are really interested and feel like flushing your brains out, read the manual, which provides the complete nuts and bolts assembly of the program and all the tricks it can do for you.

This **QUICKSTART** instruction is just another example of making it all much simpler for the average user . . . long may it continue . . . .

A cheap and useful package is the " works " program, where software houses provide you with a 3 or 4 in one, a word processor, a database, a spreadsheet and sometimes a communication module to let you talk to another P.C. with

17

a link up on a British Telecom Line. Microsoft Works and
Lotus Works are just two of many.

By the way . . . . did you know that all the
data (information) which your P.C. reads from the
program " floppy " disk, or disks in order to run it, is
in the form of separate FILES ? Files of instructive
information for the P.C.'s innards, all with their own
separate filenames.

for example . . JETSET.EXE or SYMBOLS.FNT

There can be any amount of files, who knows ? it all
depends on the size of the program.

NOW YOU KNOW !

and you will learn about FILENAMES in PART 111

A LITTLE SNIPPET

On the keyboard there are a row of keys called FUNCTION
KEYS, they are easily recognised, F1, F2, F3, F4, and so
on. Programmers and software designers use these keys to
allow you to give or receive special instructions for
that particular program.

There appears to be no standardisation other than F1,
which is the HELP key in most programs if you are
needing assistance. Pressing that will display advice on
the monitor screen and hopefully resolve your problem.

ON - LINE

Refers to a piece of hardware that is set up and ready to receive information sent to it from a particular source.

In the P.C. world it usually refers to the operational state of the printer, a little button or switch on the printer allows you to on-line it with the P.C. or off-line it, in which case the printer will stop printing.

Not Printing ? Is your printer on-line ? Check it out.

(before you say the printers faulty !)

A WORD ABOUT PRINTERS

A Personal Computer without a printer is like a pavement artist on a rainy day ! A waste of time.

Using all the tricks and programs of the computer to sort out your sales ; refunds ; stock requirements ; type out business letters etc, without being able to put it on paper is just . . . . . as I've said, a waste of time.

The basic workhorse of the printer world is the Dot Matrix printer, 9pin and 24pin, in fact 24 pin is now the "norm ", and is an *impact printer* (something like a typewriter). If you are looking for a printer that will keep your business running costs low, because of the volume of paperwork being generated, then this is the one, as it is also the cheapest to purchase and the disposable cassette ribbons don't cost an arm and a leg !

THE BUBBLEJET / DESKJET

Getting more common now in the last 3 years, this method of printing gives you laser like quality at half the price. Squirting small jets of ink onto the paper, the blacks in larger area's of graphic printouts are really dense. The selling point forbye the above is that they are very quiet in operation, and are now available in a portable battery (chargeable) version, an ideal mate for the Laptop portable P.C. These printers use a disposable ink cartridge which lasts a fair old time, although a lot dearer than the ribbon type. There are companies now selling " No Mess " ink refills for these cartridges.

THE LASER.

The daddy of the lot, but they cost, so it's all about the economics in your use of the P.C. Excellent graphics like the bubblejet, in fact excellent everything. If you can afford to buy a good quality one, then running off 86 copies of anything is not going to cost you sleepless nights. Some companies are now in the market place selling re-charged toner cartridges for these printers, giving a considerable saving over new.

THE POSTSCRIPT

These are for the serious Desk Top Publishing people and do more tricks than a performing seal. They also cost, so start putting your £1 coins in a very large jar !

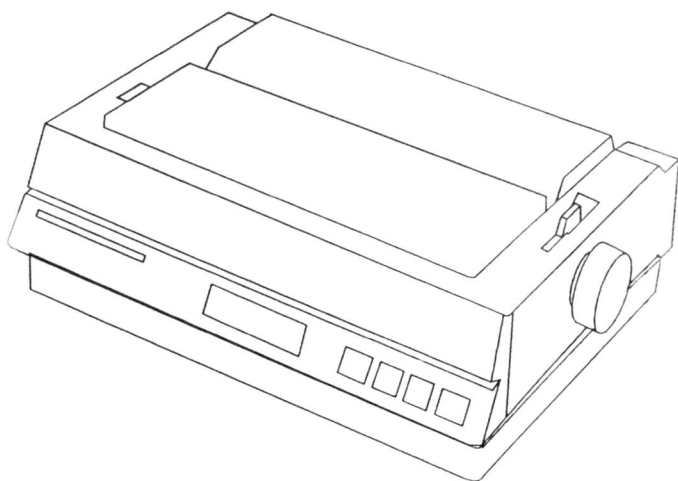

Dot Matrix Printer

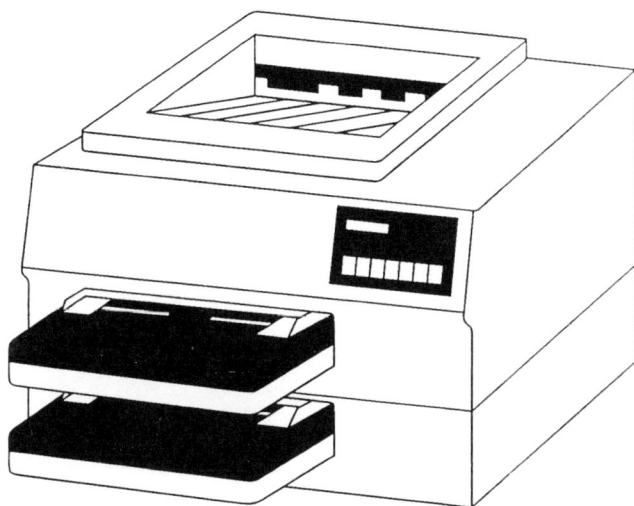

Laser Printer

PART II

The nitty gritty bit !

Understand this and you won't just break
the door down , you will demolish your
fear about using the Personal Computer

HERE WE GO . . . NICE AND SLOW.

First you must understand that the Personal Computer is
right at this moment being developed in terms of
technical innovation and design.

In fact its development is proving very similar to the
domestic video recorder sitting there beside your T.V. !
When they first appeared in the late 70's, they were much
larger in size, the de-luxe models even had timers on
them would you believe, and some manufacturers used
mechanical function keys ! Now have a look at them, some
require a university degree to operate them along with
their remote handset, but don't lose sight of their basic
function . . . .to record and play back video information
(a picture) and sound on a customised cassette. The
rest is purely gizmo's, bells and whistles. We even had
at least 4 different concepts used by manufacturers, the
two most common systems being VHS and BETAMAX. A classic
example of providing the same end result by different
means. We've recently had the same development nonsense
with satellite television, where we have had, until
recently, two separate systems, and now one has emerged
victorious. Its all about money isn't it, because a lot
of good ones have fallen by the wayside.

Let me tell you that the modern P.C. has had its moments
as well, but thankfully its system concept has been well
received and is reasonably stable, (although it's still
got some shortcomings,) The P.C. itself has made massive
gains into being accepted by the business community in
this country, and its use is spreading very quickly,
and whereas other manufacturers have made their name in
the leisure concept of computing and another has till
recently, held the undisputed crown in the field of Desk
Top Publishing, the modern P.C. has not isolated itself
by carrying out purely business applications . . . . just
witness the software (programs) now available for them.

ARE YOU READY ?

(this is the nitty gritty bit you must understand so you
can take this particular dog for a walk instead of the
other way round . . . . . .if you can understand this
lesson the rest is all downhill, so take your time.)

I'm going to repeat this twice. O.K.

*Switch on your P.C.   Unless it has a special program
called Disk Operating System in it, nothing will happen
for you !   IT WONT TALK TO YOU . YOU CAN'T TALK TO IT.*

Switch on your P.C. Unless it has a special program called Disk Operating System in it, nothing will happen for you ! IT WONT TALK TO YOU . YOU CAN'T TALK TO IT.

You can kick it, kiss it, offer it money, but it won't want to know !

When someone arranges the purchase and installation of a P.C. the dealer will sell him or her this special program, (called **DOS by every man and his dog**) some give it free as part of the sale, and most of them will have already installed it on the Hard Disk for you,(more about that later,) in that case it's advisable to make a back - up floppy disk copy of it, and don't say I didn't warn you.

Now, the P.C. in front of you, although a brilliant piece of equipment, is absolutely worthless and of no value unless you can tell it what to do and being a very logical fellow, will only listen to your commands one at a time . . .O.K. says you . . how do you talk to it ? Well the keyboard is an obvious answer, except is this P.C. thing going to understand your brand of English ? after all there are many words in the English language used in London which people in Aberdeen will pronounce and sometimes spell differently, so a *standardisation of language and commands had to be a priority.*

This is one of the problems International Business Machines (IBM) solved in the conception of the Personal Computer. They brought about the **Disk Operating System**. **DOS** is a **special program** that will manage and control all the internal and external bits of P.C. hardware to allow them to " talk " to each other and of course lets you use a " Floppy Disk " instead of huge reels of tape (as in mainframe commercial computers).

Without **DOS** installed and running in your P.C. no other programs will work . . . . It's that simple ! It allows you to control the disk drives on your P.C. and all the data you record or play from them, allows the Printer to get all the information you've just typed on the monitor screen so it can print it, makes sure the monitor shows you exactly what you are doing etc, and more importantly **gives you the simple words of command that the P.C. can understand.**

Obviously since 1980 DOS has undergone modifications, updates and changes, witness the version numbers after the initials DOS ! till at version 3.3 the command language is quite extensive, which is the part of the learning curve that most people find boring and difficult, that and the set way of typing in the commands from the keyboard. (called **syntax,** by the way)

DOS version 4 brought about the biggest breakthrough in the " user friendly " approach, because let's face it something had to be done, feedback from the " workface " was telling the people that matter, *" the quantum leap in sales that you keep dreaming about, is a " no go ", because the average operator is not interested in screwing his or her brains in and out 5 days a week trying to remember the DOS command language and the format of typing it in ! and, if mr or mrs joe public is ever to have one in their home, they will certainly give it " the bums rush " !*

This breakthrough was the **DOSSHELL**, (the DOS shell) a real gigantic step in making the P.C. easier to use. All those command words and set typing phrases that gave you the *" heeby jeebys "* trying to remember, were now being hidden " behind " a graphic display on your monitor screen showing you " **menu** " bars with the command words in plain English.   All you had to do was move a little arrow about the monitor screen, with the aid of a piece of hardware called " **a mouse** ", point it at the command word, click a button on the " mouse ", and Hey Presto, the command was carried out.

Easy Peasy !

Since then **DOS 4.1** has arrived and currently we have DOS 5 . . . .   6, 7, 8, 9, who knows ? but improvements in making work easier are always welcome. aren't they ?

The latest innovation in the *make it easier* category is, instead of the colourful graphic displays with " menu " bars in English, is an equally colourful display showing little icon squares (bit pictures) describing the commands or functions, this means that you can *talk* to this thing even if your an Eskimo living in Glasgow !

Now the command language can be increased or refined if it wants, 'cause just by selecting a little picture, and "clicking" a mouse, this P.C. thing will dance on a string for you.

A POTTED HISTORY OF DOS

1981 ish	DOS version 1	Very limited as P.C.'s were using a single sided disk, 160 k/byte of data only and the command language used few words.
	DOS version 1.1	Update of version 1 and gave support to double sided disks.
1983 ish	DOS version 2	This is really when the disk operating system started to move because of the faster P.C. (new silicon chips and new technology), also the command language was increased and the Hard Disk controlled.
1984 ish	DOS version 3	The IBM PC/AT arrived on the scene, a real fast computer, in all its functions, especially using the hard disk and the higher capacity 5¼ diskettes, networking management was catered for in this version.
1985 ish	DOS version 3.2	Update on version 3 to to support the new 3½ "floppy" disks and the drive. twice as much data as a standard 5¼ Disk.
1987 ish	DOS version 3.3	Introduced to support the IBM PS/2 computer series, and the **higher capacity** 3½ inch disk (1.44 m/byte) and its drive, at this point international support increased to around 15 countries and with it a new character set.

1990 ish	DOS version 4	Introduced the dosshell and with it all manner of attendant graphics, making it easier for the operator to use.
	DOS version 4.1	An update of version 4, which is a nice way of saying " we've looked at it again and sorted out some of the bits we weren't happy with ! "
1991 ish	DOS version 5	The DOS program itself uses up valuable P.C. memory to run it, this version brings about the same results using less memory, therefore releasing more for the operators use.

" ish ", simply means, roughly about !

If you want to know the exact dates,

though I can't think why ? ask your

office genius !

A LITTLE SNIPPET

 International Business Machines (I B M), have their
own version of the Disk Operating System . . . .

       CALLED . . . . **P.C. DOS.**

All other manufacturers, *and there are many*, who use
IBM's concept in Personal Computers have a Disk Operating
System developed by the Microsoft Corporation . . .

       CALLED . . . . **M.S. DOS.**

as far as you are concerned, there is complete
compatibility in the systems, if I have an IBM P.C. and
you have an Olivetti P.C., we can swap disks and they
will run on either machines. The difference is purely
technical and is of no interest to you as an operator,
I assure you.

But some *knowall* will talk about it, so it's just as well
for you to know, ... *now you can nod your head !*

Booting Up ?

Curious phrase, but the *office genius* will use it, of
that I have no doubt, sounds good to people that know
nothing about P.C.'s.

Let me explain . . . .

Our old friend DOS, as I'm sure you will agree must start
to run inside your computer when you switch on, O K ?
Now, in order for this to happen, a special circuit
inside the computer causes DOS to start running as soon
as you switch on the P.C. This special circuit is called
ROM (read only memory) it " **boots up** ", or to use
plain language, *starts up*, the Disk Operating System
program, and at this point . . . .

DOS simply makes your P.C. come alive.

Otherwise, no electronic bits that make up the modern
Personal Computer will " talk " to each other, that means
you can't control the disk drives, the monitor will not
show you your program, the keyboard won't display its
characters on the screen, etc . . . .

A very special program indeed, nothing more, which the
P.C. can arrange to run from your Hard Disk or the " A "
Drive (if you want to use the original program disks.)

**I'm 99.99% sure the dealer will have installed it on the
hard disk, *because*, it's then run automatically for you.**

How your Personal Computer does this is quite simple.
There is a special memory circuit in your computer called
READ ONLY MEMORY, (known as **ROM** to the whole world !)
Now this **ROM** contains a special set of instructions which
allows electronic circuits to read the **DOS Program
Instruction Files,** (these files are in the DOS program)
and having read them , instructs the P.C. to run the DOS
program from the Hard Disk. Just like that !

Remember I explained to you how all programs are made up
of FILES of instructive information or data ?

Well two of the most important files in the DOS program
are the **CONFIG.SYS** FILE (jargon for the configuration
of the system file) and the **AUTOEXEC.BAT** FILE
(will automatically carry out your instructions file)
so by typing in particular instructions or data to these
two files the P.C. and DOS will start off displaying or
doing anything you want it to !

(The **.SYS** and **.BAT** filename extensions are special
extensions used in the P.C.'s operating system.)

Let him or her preen their feathers of knowledge while
you smile.

(comes from the old " bootstrap " circuits in the early
computers, and once again, you don't want to know,   I
assure you ! nice phrase though.

A LITTLE SNIPPET

To **RE - BOOT** your system, (like switching your P.C. on
from scratch again) Hold down the **CTRL** and **ALT** keys,
whilst hitting the **DELETE** key . . .
    Saves your ON / OFF switch from wearing out !

NOW'S THE TIME . . .

Your P.C. has a little clock inside it, which is kept
going by a re - chargeable battery inside the computer.

This little clock allows the P.C. to keep a track of the
exact date and time, and is used by the computer as a
reference for different things, so when your P.C. is all
connected up and working . . . you will be asked to set
it up in accordance with the manufacturers instructions.

An example of its use . . . . if you buy a typing tutor
program or perhaps a game, you might have to complete a
module or race, *against the clock*, then the program, to
make *its* timing or clock accurate will synchronise itself
with the P.C. clock while it runs.

This re - chargeable battery gets " topped up " by a
little charging circuit which runs off the mains input of
the P.C.

Leave your P.C. unplugged for a long time and you run the
risk of this battery cell discharging, with the result
that you will have to set the date and time again.

PART III

USING IT !

" I'm stuck, I'm stuck ", you groan and at that point the office genius appears, will elbow you to the side of your seat, hit what seems like 20 keys on the keyboard and say " there you are " !

As sure as little green apples . . . .

Two or three years ago that Part III heading would have
been the scenario for you, 'cause you might have
forgotten some of the DOS commands or messed up the
special way to type them in on the keyboard, but thanks
to the dosshell and DOS 4, which supports the use of the
mouse, its simply a case of pointing an arrow at the
command word and BINGO ! it happens for you.

NOW . . .

Can I tell you in kiddywink language how to sit down in
front of this Personal Computer thing and operate it
right away ? The short answer is , well , mmm , maybe !

Let me explain that answer using a little story . . .

I've just given you the keys of a Ford Escort motor car !
You tell me you have never driven a car in your life, but
after about 2 or 3 weeks instruction you feel confident
and are pleased with your new found driving skills.

So what would you say if I suddenly gave you the keys to
a Jaguar XJ6 automatic saloon ? Oh dear, I can hear you
say, Automatic ? what's that ? where is the clutch
pedal ? the other car had 3 pedals this one only has 2 !
Why is the gearstick different ? and so on . . .

It's a silly scenario, but as in the motor car world, so
in the P.C. world . . many different makes all with their
own little design features, but just as both cars have a
petrol tank, 4 wheels, a steering wheel, wiper blades, an
engine etc, so the P.C 's have a monitor, a keyboard,
a box full of electronic wizardry, a power supply etc,
sure, just like the motor cars their shapes and bits
might also look a little different, **but they all follow
the same basic design format.**

I suppose it's to be expected , every one a little
different, anyway it would make for a drab world if
everything looked the same wouldn't it ? . . . .
**WELL SWITCH IT ON, at least this is one of the common
bits !**
The light emitting diodes (leds) or indicator lamps as
they used to be called in the good old days, red, green
or orange are telling you that the power supplies are
reaching the computer, the monitor, the keyboard and the
printer, (if you have switched that on as well).

A humming noise from the computer box ? it's probably
the cooling fan, keeping all the electronic bits nice and
cool.

The printer (if you switched it on) playing a funny
little tune ? It's self checking and handshaking with
the P.C.   Most do it every time they are switched on.

32

Hooray ! the monitor screen is lit up, **BUT,** what does it show you ? Now remember what I told you about the **CONFIG.SYS** FILE (configure the system file) and the **AUTOEXEC.BAT** FILE (will automatically carry out your instructions file) in the DOS program, for at that point **you could see a menu on the screen** showing you something like a b c d e f or 1 2 3 4 and opposite them a list of all your programs kept on the hard disk, then all you have to do is type the letter or number on the keyboard and the program will run. **simple !**

OR

A program like a word processor, or even a database will automatically start running as soon as you switch on, because that is all the P.C. is used for and DOS tells it to run every time the P.C. is switched on.

OR

The monitor screen shows you the **DOS PROMPT** C:> which means that the P.C. is ready and it is waiting on a command from you. In that case you will refer to the manufacturers " HOW TO USE YOUR P.C. " operating manual or purchase a " TEACH YOURSELF DOS " book ! Why ?

In the past, the horrors of the DOS prompt gave many operators an excuse to take up oil painting or other leisurely pursuits !, rather than get embroiled in the DOS command language, typing in a set format of instruction, loading program disks in and out a dozen times a day, changing directories and drives and so on. Thankfully these days are slipping away very fast now as the new generation of Personal Computers and programs offer **visual** operating techniques.

Your dealer or technician can set up your P.C. to suit your way of working, it's simple for him to do and won't cost you an arm and a leg ! Reputable dealers test your P.C. before dispatch or delivery, install the DOS program, and any other programs you wish to purchase, they will also set up the **CONFIG.SYS** FILE and **AUTOEXEC. BAT** FILE in the DOS program to start the P.C. in an easy to use manner, suitable for selecting your chosen programs when you switch on.

After that all you have to do is learn how to use your programs, and good dealers will always give you a quickstart demonstration . . . .

Finally, don't forget you also have inbuilt tutorials in some programs and a very important " how to use your P.C." manufacturers handbook as backup.

LIKE TYING YOUR SHOELACES,
NEVER FORGET THIS EITHER. . . .

*" every piece of information used in a P.C., either in
its program or typed in by you via the keyboard is
contained in a FILE."*

Having said that, there is now some information I am
going to give you, that will apply to any Personal
Computer or program you will ever use.

It stands to reason that if you " *create* " a file of
information inside a P.C. or in a program running in it,
you will have to give the file some kind of reference
number or name, **otherwise**, how can the P.C.'s system ever
find it for you when you want it ?

LET ME EXPLAIN . . .

NAMING A FILE

When you type a letter using a typewriter it is common
business practice to give it a reference, yes ? It allows
you at some future time to find it or refer to it for
whatever reason. Where do you keep it ? In a folder, and
more than likely in a filing cabinet. Well, when you
type a letter using a word processing program in your
computer it's no different, only there are a set of rules
the P.C. will require you to keep, if you don't, then it
will search and search all day and never find it for you.

Here are the golden rules . . . .

A file name can be **UP TO 8 characters long** using a
combination of the following,

A   to   Z

0   to   9

or ! @ £ $ % & ( ) - _

the letters can be lower case (small ones) or upper
case (capitals) **some** P.C.'s don't recognise any
difference in the character sizes. e.g. A letter to the
Royal Insurance can be **ROYAL1** or **royal1**

BUT   . . .

34

You can, if you wish, make an extension reference to the File that makes it even easier for you and the P.C. it's called the **File Extension**, and consists of **UP TO 3 characters following a full stop after the File name.**

Letters to the Royal Insurance can now be   **ROYAL1.LTR** royal2.1tr , ROYAL.3 or ROYAL.75   etc. . etc. . , you can make up a reference system to suit yourself. . . . . more examples,   **accounts.feb,   finance.hol,   SERVICE.CAR**

NOTE . . .   NO TWO FILES NAMES MUST EVER BE IDENTICAL.
GET   THE   IDEA ?

IMPORTANT :   You must never use .EXE .COM .BAS .BAT The P.C. system has reserved them for special purposes.

Now let me remind you again that it is not only your letters that will have to get a reference, but **ANY DATA** you type into a P.C., either separately or as part of a program format.   Also as I have mentioned before and *what causes some confusion*, is that programs themselves are made up of files of information.   THEY HAVE ALREADY BEEN GIVEN FILENAMES BY THE PROGRAM AUTHOR, AND YOU ARE ADVISED NOT TO TOUCH THEM.   **EVER, NEVER, and FORGET IT !**

The file and directory structure in a P.C. system is so important to the operator that a KIDDYWINK EXPLANATION of what it's all about is in order . . .   are you ready ?

NOW THERE ARE MANY WAYS TO DO THIS, I PREFER THIS METHOD

You have 3 programs in your computer, installed on the Hard Disk, they are . . .
1. A word processing program called " EASYWORD ".
2 A spreadsheet called   " CALC9 ".
3 A database called   " STOCK ".

Let's think now of the P.C's Hard Disk as a large filing drawer called   C:

There will be folders inside it for holding separate files of information, these folders in P.C. jargon are called **DIRECTORIES,** so, you will have a **DIRECTORY** for " EASYWORD ", a **DIRECTORY** for " CALC9 ", and a **DIRECTORY** for " STOCK ", that's all there is in the filing drawer, *3 folders or DIRECTORIES with separate files of information in them.   O.K. ?*

To save repeating myself, I will use " EASYWORD " as an example . . . . let me remind you once again that there are files *created* in the assembly of the program, by the guy or gal " what " wrote it ! so, the directory of " EASYWORD " could have 5 named files in it already, ... which are files that " want to be alone " O.K. ?

Any FILE that **you create,** such as a letter to your bank, will have to be given a name before you put it in the " EASYWORD " directory, most programs will prompt you to do so by asking you to " **SAVE AS** " or something similar.

In that case, make up a file name using the proper rules, say . . **BANK.LTR** and when your P.C. searches for it, according to the principles of DOS it will follow this path . . . .

C:\EASYWORD\BANK.LTR   see fig 1

If you want to keep your *personal* letters separate inside the directory of " EASYWORD ", then you can *create* a **SUB - DIRECTORY** from " EASYWORD " called " **PERSONAL** ", it's just like a special envelope, purely for your *personal* letters which will be kept *inside* the directory, along with all your other letters and the program assembly files, in the filing drawer (**C:**), in fact you can *create* as many sub - directories as you like, so when your P.C. searches for a personal letter you composed to friend Mary, it will according to the principles of DOS follow this path . .

C:\EASYWORD\PERSONAL\MARY.LTR   see fig 2

ALL YOU ARE REALLY DOING BY *CREATING* DIRECTORIES, SUB - DIRECTORIES AND FILENAMES IS GIVING THE PERSONAL COMPUTER AND ITS DOS PROGRAM A DEFINITE PATH TO FIND YOUR DATA OR FILE IT FOR YOU VERY QUICKLY.

ANOTHER LITTLE SNIPPET

not essential . . . . . . but nice to know !

You may possibly hear the " *office genius* " talk about the " **ROOT DIRECTORY OF C:** " all this means is the point at which the search or file path starts on the Hard Disk.

THE SEARCH AND FILE PATH, USING " EASYWORD "
AS AN EXAMPLE, showing . . . . . .

DIRECTORIES, SUB - DIRECTORY and FILES

C:\EASYWORD\BANK.LTR

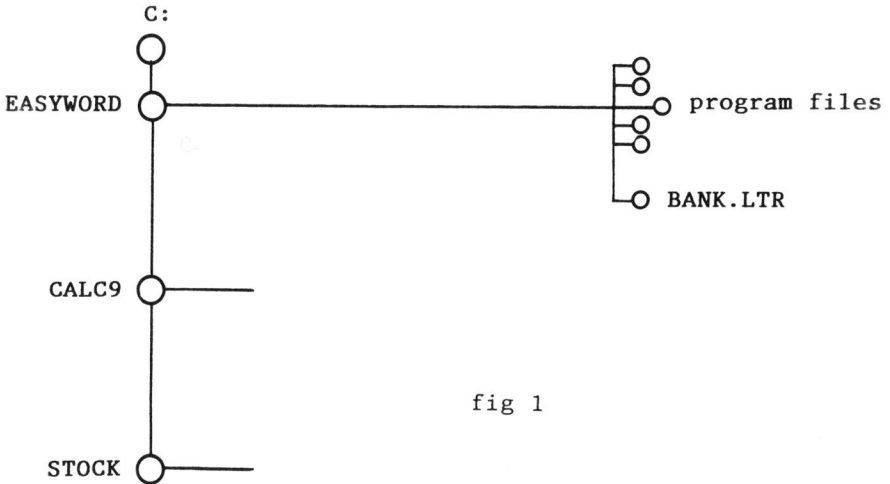

fig 1

C:\EASYWORD\PERSONAL\MARY.LTR

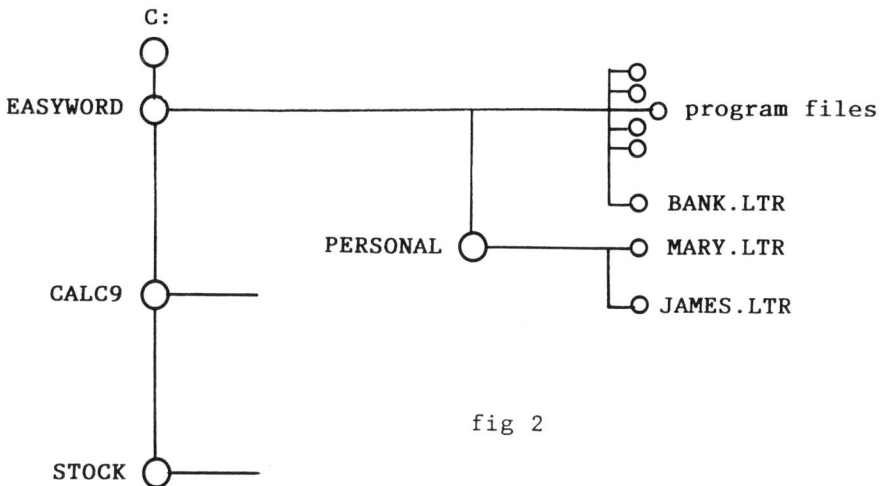

fig 2

PART IV

Bits & Bobs
and
The way ahead

THE G U I

or gooey

The way ahead for the operator . . .

Graphical User Interface.

This as I have already mentioned before, (colourful
graphic displays on your monitor screen), makes life
even easier for the operator, because already by DOS
version 3.3 an extensive vocabulary had to be learned,
and when 1990 brought the DOSSHELL and it's little arrow
activated by the " mouse ", a lot of operators thought,
" *that's it for a while* ", but no, a recently introduced
G U I program by **Microsoft** called " **WINDOWS** " arrived
on the scene, which makes the P.C. even more simple to
use !   Now in all fairness there have been other G U I,
but this one seems to have hit the bell. I suspect
improvements will be made to this just as in DOS. In
fact as I write it's **WINDOWS 3.1** !

New Programs are being written and old favourites re-
written for use in the " WINDOWS " GUI. which allows you
to look at all the DOS commands or files in your programs
in picture form, actually they are called **ICONS**, little
tiny bit-pictures which are in a special graphics display
on your monitor, so that all you have to do is point the
arrow at your selection and PRESTO ! There you have it.
You don't even need to know the language of DOS !

**Just like DOS, the G U I is a special program, and should
be installed on the Hard Disk so that it " boots up "
automatically when you switch the P.C. on, otherwise it
won't want to know !**

Also entering the *fray in the* " make it easier for the
operator contest ", is IBM with their OS/2 system. This
is actually an *inbuilt system* in their P.C.'s as opposed
to a special program.

MODEM

Means **modulator / demodulator** . . it is just a special electronic circuit that couples your P.C. up to another type of data handling system, such as using a telephone line to " talk " to another P.C. !

It plugs into the **SERIAL PORT** (an in/out data socket) on your P.C. and whatever your connecting up to.

Now you can bid the *Office Genius* " Good Modem " !

NETWORKING

The Way Ahead for the P.C.

It had to happen I suppose, P.C.'s upstairs, downstairs and all over the place.

Once the province of large multiples and companys with oodles of money and a workload to match. Networking is now becoming the "norm" for small businesses. It is the descriptive name given to connecting 2, 3, or more P.C.'s with the use of special cable forms so they can share data and use common resources such as special modems and perhaps a good quality laser printer, rather than buying 3 dot matrix types. There are different ways of doing this would you believe ? and when technical types start to plan a layout to suit your building and way of working, we enter the door of **TOPOLOGY** !   Now there's an 'ology I bet you've never heard of before ?
Topology is the study of geometrical properties. In the case of P.C. networks it means the shape of the connecting framework.

some examples . . .

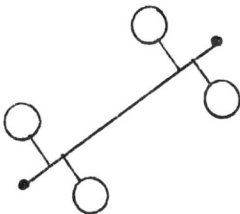

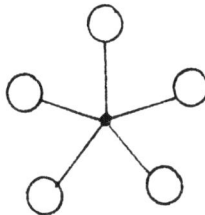

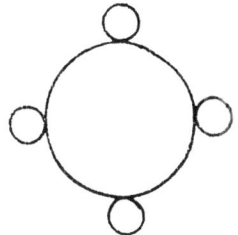

BUS   STAR   RING

Now there are many articles and dedicated publications dealing with this subject, so " dig in " if you are

interested in networking, but it's a safe bet you will
hear the *office genius* talk about . . .

1. The Server.

Quite common in the business world, this system is where
one of the P.C.'s acts as server or exchange for all the
information that the others can access to, which will
include the central database, it also means that when
two P.C.'s communicate to each other it has got to be
through the server. Its drawback is that a P.C. has to
be a dedicated server, and nothing else.

1.1 Peer to Peer system.

This type as the name suggests is when nobody and
everybody is a server ! You can all delve into each
others pockets so to speak, and use your mates printer as
well ! Gaining popularity now, as one of the benefits is
not having a P.C. as a dedicated server, and data sharing
is cheap and easy.

1.2 IBM's Token Ring system.

A robust system which can be used in a heavy workload
situation. Imagine a ring topology where a " token " is
electronically circling round the 4 or more P.C.'s all
the time. If your P.C. has something to pass on or say
to another it grabs the token, *so to speak*, sticks the
data on it, tells it the destination and off it goes !
while it's doing this no other P.C. can use the token.
don't think this takes a long time to happen, it's
extremely effective and quick in action.

Network JARGON

Node   terminals in a network
                  are called nodes

W A N   wide area network

L A N   local area network

CSM/CD   carrier sensing multiple access
                  with collision detection
                  (Just like the dodgems !)

SOME GOOD ADVICE

Always take backup copies of your work, on a daily, or at least a weekly basis if you are working with the hard disk most of the time. . . . **PLEASE** !

You never know if a fault can develop causing a loss of your programs or the data you have accumulated on the Hard Disk.

UNLIKELY ? Fair comment in todays electronics,

and

yes, you always have your original DOS program disks and all your other program disks as well, which means they can be " installed " on to the Hard Disk after the fault has been repaired.

BUT WHAT ABOUT THE INFORMATION YOU HAVE PUT INTO THESE PROGRAMS ?

Another piece of good advice is to " **save** " often whilst you are typing for a very long time, say for example, a work schedule or a 6 page contract . . . all it needs is for someone to switch off the mains supply and **your** data will all go down the plughole ! Because . . . before you " **save it** ", your data is only held in a **temporary memory** **circuit** (**called RAM**) inside the computer, whilst you are composing it.

" A gnashing of teeth ". . . .
will be mild, compared to what you'll do !

AND NOW . . .

A parting thought . .

YOU   CANNOT   BREAK   IT   !

When all is said and done, you just switch it off, wait
about 30 seconds, switch it on. Then load or select your
program and start again . . . .

**The only sadness you experience is losing the information
you have just typed in !**

I've just had a thought . . . . **now you can read
computer magazines.**

HAVE   FUN

The last of the Jargon . . . . .

Basic **Pascal** **Cobol** **Fortran** **Logo** **Forth**	These are all programming languages that the innards of computers understand, as I've said, you don't want to know, just accept that programs run on your P.C.
Microprocessor or **C P U**	This is the most important Integrated Circuit in your computer, this is the CHIP that does all the work, in a constant state of development, they are getting faster and more powerful by the months rather than years.
R A M	Random Access Memory, this is a **temporary memory circuit** which will hold the current program being used and also allow the CPU to run that program.
R O M	Read Only Memory, another memory circuit only this type is likened to Moses and the stone tablets ! Special computer management programs are written into these chips and you can't access them.
FONTS	This is where *typeface* styles are kept in your printer. Some printers offer extra font "cards" which gives you more choice.
LINE FEED	This moves your paper up one line at a time, at the end of each line of printing.
FORM FEED	This is the system whereby a contineous roll of paper is moved up to start a new page each time.
FANFOLD	Term used to describe accordion like folded paper which is fed by tractor feed into the printer, the sheets are perforated for easy separation if required.

45

PERIPHERAL	Any extra piece of equipment you can connect to your P.C.
D T P	An abbreviation for Desk Top Publishing. P.C.'s are capable of running programs which can print you a local paper ! The printer determines " quality " and size.
COMPATIBLE	Simply means, " our stuff can do anything an IBM can do ".
HANDSHAKING	Term used to describe the exchange of messages between the P.C. and other equipment indicating they are ready to receive or exchange data.
CURSOR	A symbol on your monitor screen which shows where the **next** character will be printed.
PARALLEL PORT	In/out connector socket for data, printers are usually plugged in here.
SERIAL PORT	RS232 type is the most common, your modem is connected to a serial port.
L E D	Light emitting diode, modern replacement for an indicator lamp, the advantage being no heat dissipation.
SCROLLING	When you fill up your monitor screen with TEXT, your P.C. will automatically keep moving it up to leave you space at the bottom. This can also be carried out using the mouse.
BYTE	Describes the minimum amount of Data, equivalent to you typing 2 characters on your keyboard.
CHIP	Term for an integrated circuit made from silicon.

PART V

The
"dreaded"
Class Exam !

No pat on the head . . . . no certificate

No prizes !

1. The Laptop P.C. only works from its own battery pack.

   True/False

2. You can operate a P.C. without " a mouse ".

   True/False

3. " Floppy Disks " are available in 3½ inch & 5¼ inch.

   True/False

4. High Density " floppy's " hold the most data.

   True/False

5. A " Floppy Disk " holds more data than a Hard Disk.

   True/False

6. A **DATABASE** is a program where you keep administrative records, in any arrangement, for easy access at any time.

   True/False

7. A **CENTRAL DATABASE**, is the term given to a Database program shared by other P.C.'s in a network.

   True/False

8. A **SPREADSHEET** is a drawing program.

   True/False

9. A **WORD PROCESSING PROGRAM**, used in a P.C., makes it the modern day equivalent of a typewriter.

   True/False

48

10. To Re-boot the P.C., press the **CTRL** and **ALT** keys whilst hitting the **ESCAPE** key.

True/False

11. An **ICON** is a tiny graphic bit picture.

True/False

12. The term **R A M** means Random Access Memory.

True/False

13. The term **R O M** means Reference Only Memory.

True/False

14. Filenames can be *up to* 6 characters long.

True/False

15. The filename extension is *up to* 3 characters long after a full stop.

True/False

16. The term **D O S** means Disk Operating Sensor.

True/False

17. **FILES** of data or information are kept in Directories and Sub-directories.

True/False

18. You need a **MODEM** to couple up your P.C. to another form of data handling system, e.g. using a telephone line to "talk" to another P.C. or a FAX machine.

True/False

ANSWERS OVERLEAF

ANSWERS

1.	False	10.	False
2.	True	11.	True
3.	True	12.	True
4.	True	13.	False
5.	False	14.	False
6.	True	15.	True
7.	True	16.	False
8.	False	17.	True
9.	True	18.	True

That wasn't too bad was it ?   *How did you get on ?*

All Correct ?   THEN PROCEED TO THE COMPUTER.

Some of them wrong ?   SORRY, RETURN TO PAGE 2.

ALL WRONG ?   @*&£@ !   STICK TO PEN AND PAPER !

ooOOOoo